Dedication

For Asiah and Dakotah,

Your presence in my life has been a source of joy and inspiration. You have both grown into remarkable individuals, and I am grateful for every moment we've shared.

And to little Esme,

May your journey be filled with the same love and wonder that you've brought into our lives. You are the newest chapter in our story, and we cherish every page.

With all my love,
Yvette

FRANKIE AND LOLA
ICE CREAM
DAY

Yvette M. Roman

Illustration Design by Asiah Hajicek

Hey Lola! Should we go out today? Frankie Asked.
"Ya! I think it would be so Fun!" Lola said exitedly.

"Let's get our bikes.
Helmets on because safety first."
"I will help you. Lola. Frankie said
"Ok. let's go!" Lola exclaimed.

"Wow, it's sunny and it's beautiful today, but it sure is hot." Frankie said.

"What's that sound?"
(Hearing music) Lola asked.

"Look! It's a colorful truck!" Lola called out.
"That's an ice cream truck," Frankie said.

"Let's stop and get some."
"YAY!" Lola was excited.

"I've never had ice cream but heard it's so yummy.
Oh, my goodness! It's soooo good."
Lola purred.

"I feel so much better now." Frankie said

"Ok, let's go see what else we can find today."

"Look!" Lola pointed at the lake.

"It's so beautiful."

"Let's go on the dock," Frankie said.

"Hi," said a little voice. "What's your name?"

"I'm Lola and this is Frankie, my brother.
What's yours?"

"I'm Goldie.
Will you both be my friends?"

"Of course! Let's all be friends."
Frankie replied.

"Wow, that tastes amazing. Thank you!"

"I have a small boat. We should all go for a ride."
suggested Goldie.

"Yes, let's go. I will help you in and we have life vests to keep us safe."

"I will help you with yours, Lola,
Frankie said.

Frankie, Lola, and Goldie got to go around
the lake and have Fun together.

All the while Goldie was swimming right next
to them and having a great time.

"We would love to stay, but we have to go home now. It's almost our bedtime."

"Thank you for sharing Lola and Frankie.
And becoming my new friends."

"Thank you, Goldie,
For all the Fun! We will see you again."

"Goodbye Goldie."

"What a nice day." Lola said.
"I have so much Fun with you."

"Me too, Lola." Frankie smiled.